BARRY

An Inspiring Sport Story for Kids-Discover the Life of a Legend, Icon and the Record-Breaking Champion, from Small-Town Dreams to NFL Stardom

Dale J. Gibson

Copyright

© 2025 by Dale J. Gibson. All rights reserved.

No part of this publication may be reproduced, distributed, or transmitted in any form or by any means, including photocopying, recording, or other electronic or mechanical methods, without the prior written permission of the publisher, except for the use of brief quotations in a review. The information contained in this book is intended solely for general educational use. The author has done his or her best to check the accuracy and reliability of the information within this book, but websites change frequently without notification.

Table of Contents

Chapter 1	1
Humble Beginnings	1
Chapter 2	6
High School Star	6
Chapter 3	11
College Glory at Oklahoma State	11
Chapter 4	16
Becoming a Detroit Lion	16
Chapter 5	21
The Magic of #20	21
Chapter 6	26
A True Game-Changer	26
Chapter 7	31
Life Off the Field	31
Chapter 8	36
The Shocking Retirement	36
Chapter 9	42
The Hall of Fame Journey	42
Chapter 10	48

Barry's Legacy for Kids   48

Fun Facts, Glossary and Short Quiz   53

Chapter 1

Humble Beginnings

A Boy from Wichita

Barry Sanders was born on **July 16, 1968**, in **Wichita, Kansas**, a city where hard work mattered more than anything. Life wasn't always easy, but it taught Barry important lessons early on. His father, **William Sanders**, worked as a roofer—a tough, demanding job that meant long hours under the hot sun. His mother, **Shirley Sanders**, was a homemaker, balancing care for Barry and his siblings while keeping their home running smoothly.

Barry was the **seventh of eleven children**, which meant their house was always full of energy, noise, and activity. Sometimes, Barry joked that there was never a quiet moment growing up. His brothers and sisters were his first teammates, whether they were playing games in the backyard or sharing chores around the house.

Life for the Sanders family wasn't filled with luxuries. Barry's father often reminded his kids of the value of hard work. William had a phrase he repeated over and over: **"If you want something, you've got to go out**

and get it yourself." Those words would stick with Barry as he grew older and faced new challenges.

Barry wasn't the tallest or strongest kid in his neighborhood. In fact, some of his classmates teased him about being shorter than most of the boys his age. But what Barry lacked in size, he made up for with determination and focus. Even as a young boy, he had a quiet confidence about him—a sense that he could achieve something great if he put in the effort.

Growing Up with Football Dreams

Growing up in Wichita, sports were a way of life. Boys in the neighborhood often gathered for pickup football games at the local park, and Barry was no exception. From the moment he first held a football, something clicked. He loved the feeling of running with the ball, dodging friends trying to tackle him, and scoring touchdowns.

At **Wichita North High School**, Barry began to stand out as a talented athlete. But there was a twist in his story: he wasn't always a running back. In his first two years, Barry mostly played as a **cornerback**, focusing on defense rather than offense. People barely noticed him because he didn't have many chances to show what he could do with the ball in his hands.

Even so, Barry didn't let frustration get to him. He kept practicing, believing that his time would come. His father often encouraged him, but not in the way some parents might. William didn't sugarcoat his advice. Instead, he pushed Barry to stay humble and keep working. "Don't let success get to your head," he'd say. "There's always someone out there better than you, so you've got to keep trying harder."

In Barry's junior year, everything changed. His coach decided to move him to the running back position. That decision was like unlocking a hidden door. Suddenly, Barry's natural talent for dodging defenders and running with incredible speed became clear to everyone watching. During one game, he scored **six touchdowns**, leaving the crowd in awe.

Barry's teammates and coaches began to notice his dedication. Unlike many other athletes, Barry wasn't loud or showy. He let his actions speak for him. Whether it was practicing for hours after school or studying game footage, Barry gave his all. And it wasn't just about football—Barry took his studies seriously, too. He knew that education was just as important as sports.

Lessons from Family

Barry often credited his family for teaching him the values that shaped his life. One of his biggest influences was his father, William, who had grown up during a time when opportunities were scarce for African Americans. William had learned the value of persistence and determination through his own struggles, and he wanted his children to carry those lessons forward.

William also had a unique way of motivating Barry. He didn't praise him lightly, even when Barry had a great game. Instead, he'd tell Barry things like, **"You could've done better,"** or, **"That was good, but don't get comfortable."** At the time, Barry didn't always appreciate this tough-love approach. But as he grew older, he realized it kept him grounded. His father wanted to make sure that success wouldn't go to his head.

Barry's mother, Shirley, was just as influential in her own way. She taught him kindness, patience, and the importance of caring for others. Shirley had a calm presence that balanced out her husband's tougher personality. She often reminded Barry that no matter how successful he became, treating people with respect and humility was what truly mattered.

Another important lesson Barry learned from his family was the value of teamwork. In a house with ten siblings, sharing and cooperation were a way of life. Whether it was helping with chores, looking after younger brothers and sisters, or simply finding a way to divide a pizza among eleven hungry kids, Barry learned early on that working together was key.

Even in his early years, Barry dreamed of playing professional football. Sometimes he'd watch NFL games on TV with his dad, imagining himself on the field someday. William wasn't one to shower Barry with false hope, but he did believe in his son's potential. He once told Barry, "If you want to play in the NFL, you're going to have to work harder than anyone else. Are you ready to do that?"

Barry didn't answer with words. Instead, he let his actions speak. He started spending extra hours running drills, practicing sprints, and sharpening his skills. Little did he know that all this hard work would set the stage for one of the greatest careers in football history.

Chapter 2

High School Star

Playing for Wichita North High

When Barry Sanders started high school in 1982, he attended **Wichita North High School**. At the time, Wichita North wasn't known for having a top-tier football team. They hadn't won a state championship in years, and the team struggled to find the spotlight among other schools in Kansas. However, for Barry, this wasn't a problem. He wasn't focused on fame or records—he just loved playing football.

As a freshman, Barry joined the team as a quiet, eager kid with dreams of showing what he could do on the field. But at first, things didn't go quite as planned. Barry wasn't chosen to play as a running back, the position he truly wanted. Instead, the coaches thought his smaller size would be better suited for defense, so they put him in as a **cornerback**.

Barry didn't complain. He knew the team needed him there, and he decided to work hard no matter what. Being a cornerback wasn't as glamorous as being a running back, but it gave Barry an opportunity to learn discipline and precision. These were skills he would carry with him throughout his football career.

For the first two years of high school, Barry wasn't the star of the team. In fact, he rarely touched the ball. But his quiet determination stood out. He arrived early to practices and stayed late, practicing footwork, running sprints, and studying the game. His teammates noticed his work ethic, even if it wasn't bringing him the recognition he deserved just yet.

Outside of football, Barry was just like any other high school kid. He worked hard in his classes, enjoyed time with his friends, and helped his family whenever they needed him. His father, William, continued to encourage him to stay focused on his goals. "Stay patient, Barry," William would say. "Your time will come." Barry listened. He had faith that his father's words would one day be true.

The Turning Point: Switching to Running Back

Barry's life changed during his junior year of high school in 1984. It was a cool September day when his coach, **Wayne Jackson**, decided to take a chance. Coach Jackson had been watching Barry during practices and saw something special in the way he moved. Barry wasn't the biggest or strongest player, but he had a kind of speed and agility that could outmatch anyone.

One day during a team meeting, Coach Jackson announced that Barry would get a shot at playing **running back**. The older players were skeptical. Some thought Barry was too short or too quiet to lead the team's offense. But Coach Jackson saw something they didn't: Barry had a fire inside him.

Barry's first game as a running back was against **Heights High School**, one of Wichita North's toughest rivals. The crowd packed the stands as the game began, and Barry stood on the sidelines, waiting for his turn. When his name was called to take the field, his heart pounded, but he stayed calm. This was his moment to prove himself.

On his first play as a running back, Barry took the ball and shot forward with unbelievable speed. He darted between defenders, spinning and juking past them with ease. By the time the play ended, Barry had gained 25 yards. The crowd erupted in cheers, and Barry's teammates stared in amazement.

By the end of the game, Barry had scored **three touchdowns**, helping his team to a narrow victory. From that day forward, no one questioned whether he belonged in the backfield. Barry Sanders was officially the team's star running back.

Making His Mark in High School

Barry's final two years at Wichita North High were nothing short of remarkable. As a junior, he carried the team on his back, rushing for more than **1,000 yards** and scoring over **10 touchdowns**. His explosive runs became the highlight of every game. Fans began packing the stands just to see Barry play.

But despite his personal success, the team still struggled to win games. Wichita North had a tough schedule, and many of their opponents were bigger and stronger. Barry didn't let this get him down. For him, every game was an opportunity to get better. His father often reminded him, "The only thing you can control is how hard you work." Barry took that to heart.

During his senior year in 1985, Barry reached a new level of greatness. In one game, he rushed for an astonishing **274 yards** and scored **four touchdowns**, leading Wichita North to an upset victory against a heavily favored team. Word about Barry's talent spread quickly, and people started calling him one of the best high school players in Kansas.

Despite his incredible performances, Barry remained humble. He wasn't the kind of player to celebrate excessively or boast about his achievements. Instead, he credited his teammates for helping him succeed. "I can't do it alone," Barry often said. "Football is a team game."

Barry's time at Wichita North wasn't without challenges. Some games were tough, and there were moments when he doubted himself. But through it all, he kept pushing forward. His teachers noticed his determination, not just on the football field but in the classroom as well. One teacher described Barry as "quiet but focused—a kid who always gave his best."

By the end of his high school career, Barry had rushed for nearly **2,500 yards** and scored **27 touchdowns**. His remarkable performances earned him **All-State honors**, but even with all his success, college scouts weren't knocking down his door. Many coaches thought he was too small to succeed at the next level.

Barry didn't let the doubters bother him. He was used to being underestimated. Wichita North High had given him the chance to shine, and he was ready to carry the lessons he learned there into the next chapter of his life.

As Barry graduated in 1986, he knew his football journey was far from over. He still had more to prove, more records to break, and more people to inspire. But no matter where his future would take him, Wichita North High would always be the place where it all began.

Chapter 3

College Glory at Oklahoma State

Joining the Cowboys

When Barry Sanders graduated from Wichita North High in 1986, his future in football was still uncertain. Despite his impressive stats and undeniable talent, many college football programs weren't convinced he could make an impact. At just 5'8" tall and weighing about 180 pounds, Barry didn't fit the mold of a typical college football player. Big schools like Nebraska and Oklahoma overlooked him.

But there was one school that saw his potential: **Oklahoma State University**. Barry caught the attention of **Oklahoma State's running backs coach, Gill Byrd**, who had been tracking his performances. Gill believed Barry's speed, agility, and work ethic could make him an asset to the team, and he convinced the school to give Barry a scholarship.

In 1986, Barry arrived in **Stillwater, Oklahoma**, to join the **Oklahoma State Cowboys**. The team already had an established running back, **Thurman Thomas**, who was one of the best in the country. This meant that Barry would spend most of his first two years playing a backup role, sitting on the sidelines, and waiting for his chance to shine.

For some players, this might have been frustrating. But Barry didn't see it that way. He used his time as a backup to study the game and learn from Thurman. During practices, Barry worked harder than anyone else. He focused on improving his speed and footwork, and he watched hours of game footage to understand how the best players found success.

By 1987, Barry's hard work was paying off. He began contributing as a **kick returner**, a position that showcased his quickness and creativity. During one game against **Texas A&M**, Barry returned a kickoff for an 83-yard touchdown. The crowd erupted in cheers as Barry dashed past defenders with incredible speed, making it look almost too easy.

Barry's coaches knew they had something special on their hands. Even though he was still a backup, his time was coming, and everyone could see it.

The Record-Breaking Heisman Season

In 1988, Thurman Thomas graduated and went on to play in the NFL, leaving Barry as Oklahoma State's starting running back. Many people wondered if Barry could live up to the expectations, but Barry wasn't worried. He had spent two years preparing for this moment, and he was ready to prove himself.

From the very first game of the season, Barry was unstoppable. In the season opener against **Miami of Ohio**, he ran for **178 yards** and scored **two touchdowns**. But this was just the beginning. Week after week, Barry put on jaw-dropping performances.

Against **Kansas State**, he rushed for an unbelievable **320 yards** and scored **five touchdowns**. A few weeks later, in a game against **Wyoming**, he rushed for **332 yards**, breaking the school's single-game record. Barry made it look effortless as he weaved through defenders, dodging tackles and outrunning everyone on the field.

By the middle of the season, it was clear that Barry wasn't just a good player—he was a once-in-a-generation talent. The media began calling him the best player in college football, and fans packed stadiums to see him in action.

One of Barry's most memorable games came against **Oklahoma**, Oklahoma State's biggest rival. In front of a crowd of over 75,000 fans, Barry put on a show, rushing for **215 yards** and scoring three touchdowns. Although the Cowboys didn't win the game, Barry's performance cemented his reputation as the most exciting player in the country.

By the end of the 1988 season, Barry had broken record after record. He rushed for an incredible **2,850 yards** in just 12 games, the most in a single season in college football history. He also scored **44 touchdowns**, an unheard-of feat.

Barry's achievements earned him the **Heisman Trophy**, awarded to the best player in college football. At the ceremony in December 1988, Barry stood on stage holding the iconic trophy, a smile on his face. It was a proud moment for him and his family, who had always believed in his potential.

But even as he celebrated, Barry stayed humble. When reporters asked him about his success, he gave credit to his teammates and coaches. "I couldn't have done it without them," he said. "Football is a team sport, and I'm lucky to have had the support of everyone around me."

The Road to the NFL

After his historic season, many wondered what Barry would do next. As a junior, he still had one year of college eligibility left. But with his Heisman-winning performance, it was clear that Barry was ready for the next level: the **National Football League (NFL)**.

Barry decided to declare for the **1989 NFL Draft**, a decision that thrilled fans but saddened Oklahoma State supporters, who wished he could stay for one more year. Still, everyone understood that Barry's future lay in the NFL.

The **Detroit Lions** selected Barry as the third overall pick in the draft. Their coach, **Wayne Fontes**, was thrilled to have Barry on the team, calling him a "game-changer." The city of Detroit was buzzing with excitement, eager to see what their new running back could do.

Before heading to Detroit, Barry took a moment to reflect on his journey. He thought about the early days in Wichita, when he was just a kid running around with a football. He remembered his father's words about hard work and his mother's constant encouragement. He thought about his time at Wichita North High, where he first discovered his talent, and at Oklahoma State, where he became a legend.

Barry's college career had been nothing short of extraordinary, but it was just the beginning. The NFL awaited, and Barry was ready to take on the challenge. Little did anyone know, his professional career would be just as legendary as his time in college.

Chapter 4

Becoming a Detroit Lion

Draft Day Dreams

The year was **1989**, and Barry Sanders was about to experience one of the biggest moments of his life: the **NFL Draft**. It was a chance for college players to take the next step and join a professional football team, but there was always a little uncertainty. Where would Barry land? Which team would take a chance on the Heisman-winning running back from Oklahoma State?

Barry wasn't the type to get caught up in all the noise. While sports analysts debated which players would go first and whether Barry was too small to succeed in the NFL, Barry stayed calm. He spent the morning with his family, sharing stories, cracking jokes, and enjoying his mother's cooking. It was just another reminder of how grounded Barry always remained.

The **draft** was held on **April 23, 1989**, in New York City. Barry and his family watched the event from the comfort of their home. The Detroit Lions had the **third overall pick**, and they were looking for someone who could revitalize their offense.

When the Lions announced their pick—Barry Sanders—cheers erupted in the Sanders household. The team's coach, **Wayne Fontes**, called Barry shortly after, welcoming him to Detroit. Fontes had high expectations for Barry, believing he could turn the Lions into a winning team.

Though Barry was excited, he also knew this was just the beginning. Getting drafted was an honor, but proving himself in the NFL would be another challenge altogether. Still, Barry was ready to take it head-on.

In Detroit, fans immediately embraced Barry. They had been longing for a superstar who could give their team new energy and excitement. "We've found our guy," some Lions fans said. For Barry, it was overwhelming but motivating. "I want to do my best for them," he told reporters during his first press conference as a Lion.

Hitting the Ground Running in the NFL

Barry joined the Lions' training camp later that summer, and right from the start, everyone could see he was something special. Even the veteran players, who had seen their share of talented rookies, were amazed by Barry's speed and agility.

Barry didn't say much during practices. He wasn't there to talk or show off—he was there to work. Every drill, every play, every run was a chance to improve. His teammates noticed how he never took shortcuts or made excuses. "Barry's quiet, but man, he's deadly with the ball," one of the veteran players remarked after a scrimmage.

The **NFL preseason** gave Barry his first taste of professional football. In his first game, Barry only played a handful of downs, but it was enough to leave fans in awe. On one play, he broke through a line of defenders and sprinted 40 yards before being tackled. Even though it wasn't an official game, Detroit fans were already falling in love with their new running back.

When the regular season began in **September 1989**, Barry's goal was simple: give his best effort every game. And in his **NFL debut** against the **Phoenix Cardinals**, he didn't disappoint. On his very first carry, Barry burst through the defense for an **18-yard run**, showcasing his incredible speed and footwork. By the end of the game, Barry had rushed for **71 yards and scored his first touchdown.**

Each week, Barry seemed to get better. Against the **Dallas Cowboys**, he rushed for **142 yards** and two touchdowns, including a dazzling 50-yard run where he left defenders grabbing at thin air. Fans couldn't believe what they were seeing. How could someone make it look so easy?

Barry's running style became a signature of his success. He had an uncanny ability to dodge defenders, making cuts so sharp it seemed like his feet were moving faster than anyone's eyes could follow. And unlike most runners who relied on brute strength, Barry relied on his speed, balance, and vision. It didn't matter if three or four defenders were chasing him—Barry always found a way to escape.

As the season progressed, Barry's name started appearing in headlines across the country. "The Lions' Secret Weapon" one paper called him. Another described him as "a human highlight reel."

Despite his personal success, Barry remained humble. After every game, he gave credit to his teammates and never took too much pride in his accomplishments. "Football is about teamwork," he said. "I just want to do my part to help the team win."

Rookie of the Year

By the end of the 1989 season, Barry had put up some astonishing numbers. He rushed for a total of **1,470 yards**—the most by any rookie that year—and scored **14 touchdowns**. His performances helped the Lions improve their record, and while they didn't make the playoffs, the team was finally headed in the right direction.

Barry's outstanding debut earned him the **NFL Rookie of the Year** award. When he accepted the honor at the NFL awards ceremony in January 1990, Barry's trademark humility shone through. He thanked his coaches, teammates, and family for supporting him, saying, "I'm just happy to play the game I love."

One of the most talked-about moments from Barry's rookie season was his final game against the **Atlanta Falcons**. Barry was just **10 yards shy of winning the NFL rushing title**, which is awarded to the player with the most rushing yards in a season. Coach Wayne Fontes offered to let Barry stay in the game and reach the milestone, but Barry declined. "The win is more important," Barry said.

That decision summed up who Barry was as a person and a player. He wasn't focused on personal glory. For Barry, football wasn't about breaking records or being the center of attention—it was about playing the game with honor and giving his best effort every time he stepped on the field.

Detroit fans knew they had something special in Barry Sanders, and they couldn't wait to see what he would do next. Barry's rookie season was just the beginning of a career that would go down in history as one of the greatest in football.

Chapter 5

The Magic of #20

Speed, Agility, and Style

When Barry Sanders stepped onto the football field, something amazing happened. His movements were unlike anyone else's, and people couldn't take their eyes off him. Wearing the **#20 jersey** for the Detroit Lions, Barry became known for his incredible **speed**, **agility**, and **style**. He turned every game into a thrilling show.

Barry's speed was out of this world. He could take off down the field so quickly that defenders often looked frozen, unable to keep up. But speed was only part of what made Barry special. It was the way he moved, cutting and dodging defenders like they weren't even there. One sports writer once said, "It's like Barry has eyes in the back of his head."

His agility was unmatched. Barry could change direction faster than anyone else. If a defender tried to tackle him, Barry would spin or juke to avoid them, leaving the defender behind. People often said it looked like Barry was dancing on the field, moving gracefully while still being incredibly effective.

But what really made Barry unique was his style. Unlike other players who powered through tackles with brute strength, Barry used his creativity and instincts to outsmart his opponents. He could take the smallest opening in the defense and turn it into a big play. Even when things looked impossible, Barry always seemed to find a way to make something happen.

Fans loved watching Barry because they never knew what he would do next. Every time he touched the ball, there was a chance for something amazing. Whether it was a 50-yard touchdown run or a play where he turned a potential loss into a huge gain, Barry kept everyone on the edge of their seats.

Memorable Games and Plays

Barry's career was full of unforgettable moments that showcased his incredible talent. One of the most talked-about games was against the **New England Patriots** in **1994**. In that game, Barry ran for **131 yards** and scored a touchdown, but it wasn't just the numbers that impressed people—it was the way he did it. On one play, Barry dodged five defenders in the backfield before breaking free for a long run. The crowd couldn't believe what they had just seen.

Another memorable moment came in **1997**, during a game against the **Chicago Bears**. Barry had one of the best runs of his career, a play that's still talked about by fans today. He took the handoff, but two defenders were waiting for him. Most players would have been tackled right there, but not Barry. He spun out of their grasp, cut to the right, then back to the left, and took off for a **40-yard touchdown**. Even the Bears' players couldn't help but admire his skill.

In **Thanksgiving Day games**, Barry was often the star of the show. One Thanksgiving in **1997**, the Lions played the **Green Bay Packers**, and Barry delivered one of the best performances of his career. He rushed for **167 yards** and scored **three touchdowns**, helping the Lions secure a big win in front of a national audience. Fans watching at home and in the stadium cheered wildly as Barry turned ordinary plays into extraordinary ones.

Perhaps the most legendary game of Barry's career came in the **1994 playoffs** against the **Dallas Cowboys**. Barry had been relatively quiet all game, but in the fourth quarter, he delivered a play for the ages. He broke free on a run that seemed impossible, zigzagging past nearly the entire Cowboys' defense to score a **47-yard touchdown**. It was a moment that cemented Barry's reputation as one of the greatest players ever.

Barry also broke records during his career. In **1997**, he became just the **third player in NFL history** to rush for over **2,000 yards** in a single season, joining O.J. Simpson and Eric Dickerson. Barry finished that year with **2,053 rushing yards**, a feat that amazed fans and critics alike. It wasn't just the yards that impressed people—it was how he got them, with dazzling runs that left defenders chasing shadows.

Inspiring Teammates and Fans

Barry's greatness wasn't just about what he did on the field—it was also about how he carried himself off it. He was quiet, humble, and respectful, qualities that earned him the admiration of his teammates, coaches, and fans.

Barry wasn't the loudest voice in the locker room, but his actions spoke louder than words. He led by example, showing his teammates that hard work and determination were the keys to success. Younger players often looked up to Barry, not just because of his talent but because of his character.

Barry's humility set him apart from many other star athletes. Even after his most amazing games, he never bragged or drew attention to himself. When asked about his success, he always credited his offensive line for blocking and his coaches for giving him the opportunity to play. "I couldn't do it without them," Barry often said.

His unselfish attitude inspired everyone around him. Teammates would push themselves harder, knowing they were playing alongside someone as special as Barry. Even players from opposing teams admired him, calling him one of the classiest players in the league.

Barry also inspired millions of fans, young and old. Kids loved watching him play because he made football fun and exciting. Many young players wanted to be like Barry, and they tried to mimic his spins and jukes in their backyard games. Parents admired him for his sportsmanship and humble demeanor, saying he was the perfect role model for their children.

Barry's impact went beyond football. He showed people that you didn't have to be the biggest or loudest person to succeed. Through his actions, Barry taught important lessons about hard work, perseverance, and staying true to yourself.

Fans in Detroit were especially proud of Barry. They hadn't had much to cheer about before he arrived, but Barry gave them hope and excitement. Every time he stepped on the field, he brought joy to the city and gave people something to rally around.

Barry's legacy as **#20 for the Detroit Lions** will forever be remembered. He wasn't just a great player—he was a once-in-a-lifetime talent who changed the game of football and inspired countless people along the way.

Chapter 6

A True Game-Changer

Breaking Records

Barry Sanders had a way of making the impossible look easy. Over the course of his 10-year NFL career, he didn't just play football—he changed the way people saw the game. One of the things that set Barry apart was his ability to break records. Every season, it seemed like he was achieving something that had never been done before.

One of Barry's most incredible records was reaching **15,000 rushing yards** faster than any other player in NFL history. By the time he retired, Barry had rushed for **15,269 yards**, placing him second all-time behind Walter Payton. But Barry's yards weren't just numbers—they were breathtaking runs that football fans would talk about for years.

Barry also set the record for the **most consecutive 1,000-yard seasons**, an achievement that showcased his consistency. From his rookie year in **1989** to his final season in **1998**, Barry ran for more than 1,000 yards every year, totaling **10 straight seasons**. This was no small feat, as every defense in the league planned their strategies around stopping him. Yet, Barry found ways to succeed.

One of his most unforgettable seasons came in **1997**, when he rushed for an astonishing **2,053 yards**. In that season, Barry became the **third player in NFL history** to surpass the 2,000-yard mark, joining an elite group that included **O.J. Simpson** and **Eric Dickerson**. What made this even more impressive was that Barry started the season slowly. In his first two games, he rushed for just 53 yards combined. After that, he went on a tear, rushing for over 100 yards in each of the next 14 games—a record-breaking streak.

Barry didn't chase records for personal glory, though. For him, each achievement was about contributing to his team's success. He rarely celebrated in flashy ways when he scored or broke a record. Instead, he calmly handed the ball to the referee, a humble act that became one of his trademarks.

10 Seasons of Excellence

Barry Sanders played for the Detroit Lions from **1989 to 1998**, and every one of those 10 seasons was filled with excellence. During a time when the Lions weren't known as a powerhouse team, Barry was their shining star, bringing excitement and hope to fans year after year.

From the very beginning, Barry showed he was different. As a rookie in **1989**, he rushed for **1,470 yards** and scored **14 touchdowns**, earning the NFL Rookie of the Year award. But Barry didn't stop there. He followed up his rookie season with another brilliant performance in **1990**, rushing for **1,304 yards** despite missing five games due to an injury.

Barry's ability to stay consistent over a decade is what truly made him special. Even in seasons when the Lions struggled as a team, Barry delivered standout performances. His runs weren't just about gaining yards—they were moments of magic that lifted the spirits of his teammates and fans.

Throughout his career, Barry earned **10 Pro Bowl selections**, meaning he was chosen as one of the best players in the NFL every single season he played. This streak is a testament to his greatness and consistency. He was also named **First-Team All-Pro** six times, further solidifying his place as one of the best running backs in history.

Barry's excellence wasn't just about statistics, though. It was also about the way he approached the game. He treated football with respect and always gave his best effort, whether it was during a big game or a routine practice. His teammates admired him for his work ethic and calm demeanor. He never made excuses and always focused on improving.

One of Barry's most remarkable qualities was his durability. Over his 10 seasons, he missed only seven games. This was incredible for a player who carried the ball as much as he did, especially considering the physical nature of his playing style. Barry always seemed to bounce back after taking a hard hit, a testament to his resilience.

Winning the MVP

The pinnacle of Barry Sanders' career came in **1997**, when he was named the NFL's **Most Valuable Player (MVP)**. This award is given to the best player in the league each year, and in 1997, no one could argue that Barry deserved it more.

The season didn't start well for the Detroit Lions. After the first five games, the team had a disappointing record of 2–3, and Barry wasn't putting up his usual numbers. Some people began to wonder if Barry's best days were behind him. But then, something incredible happened.

Starting in Week 6, Barry went on an unstoppable streak. Week after week, he ran for over 100 yards, breaking tackles, making defenders miss, and giving his team a chance to win. By the time the season ended, Barry had rushed for **2,053 yards**, becoming the **NFL's leading rusher**.

Barry's efforts helped the Lions turn their season around. They finished with a **9-7 record**, earning a spot in the playoffs. Though the team didn't go far in the postseason, Barry's performance during the regular season was unforgettable.

What made Barry's MVP award even more special was that he shared it with **Brett Favre**, the quarterback for the Green Bay Packers. It was only the third time in NFL history that two players had shared the award. While some players might have felt disappointed about not winning it outright, Barry was as gracious as ever. He expressed gratitude for being recognized and remained focused on the team.

Barry's 1997 season wasn't just about the yards or the awards—it was about the joy he brought to fans and the inspiration he gave to his teammates. Watching Barry play was like witnessing art in motion, and his MVP season was the crowning achievement of a legendary career.

Chapter 7

Life Off the Field

Staying Humble in the Spotlight

Barry Sanders was one of the most famous football players in the world, but if you met him off the field, you wouldn't know it. While other athletes enjoyed the limelight, Barry stayed as quiet and humble as the boy from Wichita, Kansas, that he had always been. Fame didn't change him, and that's what made him so special.

When Barry became a star with the Detroit Lions, he attracted attention wherever he went. Reporters wanted interviews, fans wanted autographs, and companies wanted him to promote their products. But Barry didn't act like a superstar. He avoided the flashy lifestyle that many athletes embraced. He preferred a simple life, spending his time with family, close friends, and teammates.

Barry's humility was especially clear during interviews. When asked about his accomplishments, he rarely talked about himself. Instead, he credited his teammates for their hard work. "I can't do anything without my offensive line," he often said. He also praised his coaches for helping him improve and guiding him in his career. To Barry, football was a team sport, and he didn't want all the credit.

Despite his immense talent, Barry never trash-talked other players or showed off on the field. After scoring a touchdown, he simply handed the ball to the referee and jogged back to the sidelines. It was a quiet celebration, but it spoke volumes about Barry's character. He believed the game was about respect—for your teammates, your opponents, and the fans.

Barry's humility made him a role model, not just for kids but for adults too. In a world where success often leads to arrogance, Barry remained down-to-earth. Fans admired him not only for his talent but for his kind and respectful attitude.

Supporting Causes and Giving Back

Barry Sanders used his fame and resources to help others. He didn't just want to be known as a great football player; he wanted to make a difference in people's lives. Throughout his career and even after retirement, Barry supported several causes and charities, showing that he cared deeply about giving back.

One of Barry's main focuses was helping children. He believed that every child deserved a chance to succeed, no matter their circumstances. Barry partnered with organizations like the **Boys & Girls Clubs of America**, which provides safe spaces for kids to learn and grow. He visited local chapters, spending time with the kids and encouraging them to dream big.

Education was another area Barry cared about. He worked with programs that provided scholarships and resources to students in need. He knew the value of education because it had been so important in his own life. Barry often spoke about the lessons he learned from his parents, who emphasized the importance of hard work and staying in school.

Barry also supported causes that benefited his community. In Detroit, he helped raise funds for local charities and participated in events to support the city. He understood that being a star athlete came with responsibility, and he wanted to use his platform to bring attention to important issues.

One event that stood out was a fundraiser for youth sports programs in Detroit. Barry believed sports taught valuable life lessons, such as teamwork, discipline, and perseverance. By helping kids participate in sports, Barry hoped to give them the same opportunities he had as a young boy in Wichita.

Barry wasn't one to seek attention for his charitable work. Much of what he did was behind the scenes, without press or publicity. He didn't care about being praised—he just wanted to help.

Family Life

For Barry, family always came first. Even during his football career, he made sure to prioritize time with his loved ones. He was a devoted father and husband, and his family meant everything to him.

Barry married his wife, **Lauren Campbell**, in the early 2000s. Together, they had four children: **Nate**, **Barry J.**, **Nicholas**, and **Noah**. Barry loved being a dad and took his role seriously. He wanted to be present in his kids' lives, not just as a provider but as a guide and mentor.

After retiring from football in **1999**, Barry devoted more time to his family. While many retired athletes stayed involved in the sport through coaching or broadcasting, Barry chose a different path. He wanted to be home with his wife and kids, supporting them in their pursuits.

Barry's sons inherited their father's love for sports, especially football. His oldest son, Nate, played college football at **Stanford University**, and Barry couldn't have been prouder. But Barry didn't pressure his kids to follow in his footsteps. He encouraged them to find their passions, whether in sports, academics, or other areas.

Even after stepping away from the spotlight, Barry remained close with his parents and siblings. He often visited his hometown of Wichita, spending time with his large, loving family. Barry's father, **William**, had been a huge influence on him, teaching him the value of hard work and humility. Though his father passed away in **2001**, Barry continued to honor his memory by living the values he had been taught.

Family gatherings were a big deal for Barry. He enjoyed barbecues, game nights, and just sitting around telling stories. These moments reminded him of where he came from and kept him grounded.

Barry's commitment to family didn't stop at his relatives. He saw his former teammates and friends as part of his extended family. Even after retirement, he stayed in touch with the people he had built relationships with during his career.

Chapter 8

The Shocking Retirement

Leaving at the Top

In the world of sports, one of the most surprising moments often comes when a star athlete decides to walk away while still at the top of their game. And that's exactly what happened with Barry Sanders in **1999**. For many, it felt like an unsolved mystery, like a perfect chapter in a book being torn out before anyone could finish reading it.

Barry Sanders, the electrifying running back for the Detroit Lions, shocked the world when he announced his retirement from professional football on **July 27, 1999**, just weeks before the start of the new NFL season. At the time, Barry was still in his prime. He had just finished a **1,500-yard season** and was fresh off another Pro Bowl appearance. Barry had more than enough fuel left in the tank to keep playing, so why would he suddenly quit when the whole world expected him to keep going?

To understand the impact of this decision, we have to remember where Barry stood in the game of football. By 1999, Barry had already cemented himself as one of the greatest running backs in NFL history. He had rushed for over **15,000 yards**, been selected to **10 Pro Bowls**, and collected numerous records and accolades. There was little left for Barry to prove. In fact, some football fans even started talking about Barry as possibly breaking the all-time rushing record held by **Walter Payton**—but that wasn't enough to keep Barry on the field. He knew that football, as much as he loved it, was just a part of his life.

For Barry, the most important thing was living on his own terms. He didn't want to be one of those athletes who hung around too long, staying past their prime, trying to hold on to the glory they once had. Barry didn't care about chasing records or adding extra years to his career for the sake of fans or fame. He felt he had given everything he could to the sport, and now, it was time for him to walk away while he was still at the top.

The way he left was simple yet powerful. Barry held a quiet press conference and announced that he was retiring. No grand farewell tour, no flashy speeches, just a short statement that shocked everyone who had followed his career. "I've decided to leave the game while I still love it," he said simply. No fanfare, no complaints—just a man ready to close that chapter of his life.

When you look back at Barry's retirement, it's clear that he knew his body well. He didn't want to risk playing another season and possibly losing his passion for the game, or worse, getting injured. As an athlete, you spend your career pushing your body to its limits, and Barry knew when it was time to let go. The story of his retirement is a story of self-awareness and respecting the sport.

Reactions from Fans and Friends

The day Barry Sanders announced his retirement, the world of sports came to a standstill. It was as if time itself paused for a moment, and fans everywhere couldn't believe what they had just heard. How could someone so talented, so exciting to watch, just walk away? There was a feeling of shock, sadness, and confusion in the air. Many Detroit Lions fans were devastated, as they had come to see Barry as not just a player but the heart of their team.

The fans' feelings were complicated. Some felt hurt by his decision, wondering why Barry wouldn't just play a little longer. They wanted more of those spectacular runs, more of the magic he brought to the football field every Sunday. Yet, others respected his decision. They knew that Barry had always kept his personal life private, and for him, football wasn't about making it a career that stretched out too long. Barry wanted to leave while he was still at his best.

Teammates and friends had mixed emotions as well. Some were shocked, while others said they understood. They knew how much football meant to Barry, and they respected his decision. Some even said they had a feeling

Barry might retire early. His calm demeanor and focus on his family life had given hints that he might not have the typical career span many of his peers had.

Players like **Lions quarterback Scott Mitchell** and fellow running back **Lomas Brown** were among those who expressed their surprise. They had hoped to continue playing alongside Barry for years to come, but they also understood the tough decision he had made. In interviews, Lomas Brown mentioned that Barry was a rare athlete who didn't let his fame get to his head. "He always wanted to do things his way," Brown said.

Even coaches like **Marty Mornhinweg**, who had only worked with Barry for a brief time, respected the decision. Barry was his own man, and the coach appreciated the respect Barry had for the game. It wasn't just a business decision for Barry—it was about making sure he left football with his love for the game still intact.

Though there were many fans who wanted to see Barry stay longer, they could not deny that it was hard to be upset with the reason behind his decision. He wasn't retiring because of injury or frustration with the game—he retired because he wanted to preserve the joy he found in football.

Even fans from opposing teams had to acknowledge the greatness of Barry Sanders. His farewell was met with an outpouring of respect from all corners of the NFL. **Emmitt Smith**, who was the league's all-time rushing leader, paid tribute to Barry. Smith said that he respected Barry's decision and recognized how amazing he had been to watch on the field. It wasn't just Detroit fans who loved Barry—football fans everywhere had learned to appreciate him, even if they didn't root for his team.

Why Barry Walked Away

So, why did Barry Sanders retire at the peak of his career, when he was still playing at a level most people could only dream of? The answer to that question is complex and personal, but there are a few key reasons why Barry decided it was time to leave.

First and foremost, Barry retired because football, as much as he loved it, didn't define who he was. Throughout his life, Barry always said that his identity was built on more than his performance on the field. Football was part of him, but it wasn't everything. Off the field, he was a family man, a community leader, and someone who cared deeply about his loved ones.

Second, Barry had a unique understanding of his body. While many athletes push themselves to the limit, Barry knew when to stop. After several intense seasons and endless hard work on the field, he didn't want to risk an injury that could take away the joy he had in the game. Walking away while his body was still in top condition seemed like the smart choice to him.

Barry also retired because he wanted to be in control of his own narrative. Many athletes stick around to chase records, hoping to extend their careers and break new records. Barry didn't play football for fame or personal achievements. He played the game for the love of it. And when it no longer gave him the same joy, Barry chose to step away rather than continue just for the sake of playing.

But most importantly, Barry retired because he wanted to preserve his passion for football. He wasn't the type to stretch out his career and risk growing tired of the game. For him, football had been a thrill ride, and he wanted to make sure he walked away on his own terms, knowing he had given it all he had. It was a decision not many athletes have the courage to make, but it was one that cemented Barry's place as not just an incredible player but as someone who understood what was important in life.

Barry Sanders' retirement marked the end of an era for the Detroit Lions and for the NFL. Fans will always wonder what more Barry could have done if he had played a few more seasons. However, his retirement is one of the most memorable moments in sports history because Barry Sanders showed the world that sometimes the greatest players are the ones who can walk away with grace, knowing when their time is up.

Chapter 9

The Hall of Fame Journey

What It Means to Be a Legend

Imagine walking into a room filled with the greatest football players ever. All of these athletes have made history in their own way, and in the center of that room, there's one special spot reserved for people who have given everything to the game—those who have played so well that they are remembered forever. This room is known as the **Pro Football Hall of Fame**, located in Canton, Ohio, where the legends of football are honored.

Barry Sanders earned his place in that room when he was inducted into the Hall of Fame in **2004**. His journey to that moment, however, wasn't just about the trophies, touchdowns, and records. It was about his commitment to being the best on the field while remaining true to himself off the field. Being called a "legend" is a big deal. It's not just because of your skills on the field; it's also about the impact you have on the game and how you inspire others.

When people think of legends, they think of people who seem almost larger than life, like superheroes. But Barry Sanders was different. He wasn't someone who grabbed attention with flashy celebrations or loud speeches. Instead, Barry was a man who let his feet do the talking. On the field, he dazzled with moves that left defenders looking lost, all while running at top speed with the ball in his hands. Yet, off the field, Barry's quiet nature and humility were the reasons why he stood out.

Becoming a legend takes time and dedication. It's about the constant commitment to get better, to keep pushing no matter what, and to make a lasting impact on the people you touch. For Barry Sanders, that legend status wasn't something he was chasing—it was a result of the way he lived his life and played the game.

But being in the Hall of Fame isn't about trophies; it's about legacy. It's about earning respect, and after all the years Barry spent as one of the most exciting and unstoppable forces in football, the Hall of Fame was where his story would live forever.

Honored Among the Greats

When Barry was inducted into the Pro Football Hall of Fame in **2004**, it was one of the most special moments in the history of the NFL. Being chosen to be among the greats of the game wasn't just a personal accomplishment—it was a celebration of everything Barry had given to the sport. Barry was surrounded by family, friends, former teammates, and some of the biggest names in football. But none of this mattered more to him than the feeling of being among the legends—the athletes who had helped shape the game into what it was.

Being in the Hall of Fame means that you've reached the peak of your sport, and for Barry, it was a recognition that everything he had worked for, everything he had put into football, had paid off. That day in **2004** was an emotional one, and Barry reflected on his journey. After he took his spot on the stage, he spoke humbly about his path to greatness. Like always, Barry didn't brag about the records, the amazing plays, or the highlight reels that had become so famous. He talked about his love for football, his teammates, and how fortunate he was to have been able to play the game at such a high level.

"I owe everything to my teammates and coaches," Barry said as he smiled and gazed out at the crowd. He mentioned people who had supported him from his early days in Wichita, Kansas, to his college years at Oklahoma State, to his time in Detroit as a Lion. Barry's speech wasn't about him. It was about the people who helped him reach this incredible moment. It was an opportunity to thank those who had been with him along the way.

The Hall of Fame induction ceremony isn't just about recognition—it's about looking back at a player's career and the impact they had on the sport. In Barry's case, it was about looking at how his style of play changed the running back position forever. Coaches, fans, and players all agreed that Barry's ability to cut and accelerate was unlike anyone else. Watching Barry Sanders run with the ball was like watching an artist create a masterpiece, full of twists, turns, and breathtaking moves.

Being surrounded by players like **Jim Brown**, **Walter Payton**, and **Emmitt Smith**—names that many people look up to when they think of football legends—was a humbling experience for Barry. Yet, he never seemed to let it go to his head. Instead, he continued to treat this honor the way he treated everything else in his career—with quiet confidence and humility. The Hall of Fame wasn't about proving anything—it was the recognition of all that Barry had accomplished in a career that spanned only **10 years**, but had left a mark on the NFL that would last forever.

Lessons from a Hall of Famer

What can we learn from Barry Sanders, a man who spent so many years dazzling on the football field but remained so humble off it? Barry's story has taught countless lessons—lessons that go far beyond the game of football.

1. Be Yourself: Barry was never flashy. He didn't try to outshine others with showy celebrations or personal publicity stunts. He let his game speak for itself. What can we learn from Barry's example? It's okay to be unique.

You don't have to follow the crowd or act in a certain way just to get attention. Like Barry, staying true to who you are will eventually earn you the respect of others, even if you're not trying to be noticed.

2. Hard Work Pays Off: Throughout his career, Barry worked tirelessly to be the best at what he did. He knew it took time, dedication, and sacrifice. But he loved football, and all the hard work paid off in the end when he became one of the most respected players to ever play the game. This teaches us that success isn't instant, but it comes with consistent effort and persistence.

3. Humility Matters: Even though Barry was one of the best athletes in the world, he never let his success make him arrogant. He always remained humble and never let his fame or wealth change who he was. In a world where people sometimes let popularity define them, Barry was a reminder that true greatness comes with humility.

4. Know When to Step Away: Barry's decision to retire in the prime of his career taught everyone an important lesson about knowing when to move on. He didn't push himself past his limits. He didn't hold on to something just because it was expected of him. Instead, he made his decision for his own happiness. Knowing when to step away and let go can be just as important as knowing when to give it your all.

5. Play the Game the Right Way: On the field, Barry played for the love of the game. He didn't do it for money or fame. He did it because he loved football and wanted to be the best. His dedication to doing things the right way, with respect for his teammates, coaches, and the sport itself, left a lasting legacy for generations to come.

As fans filled the Hall of Fame and celebrated Barry Sanders' achievements, they didn't just remember him for his stats or his running moves. They remembered him for how he changed the game and how he played with a passion and respect that made him one of the greatest running backs of all time. The Pro Football Hall of Fame isn't just a place to honor great athletes; it's a place to remember those whose work ethic, humility, and commitment made an impact that goes beyond football. Barry Sanders' induction wasn't just about football—it was about life, respect, and doing the best you can every day.

Chapter 10

Barry's Legacy for Kids

Hard Work and Perseverance

If there's one thing Barry Sanders' life and career taught us, it's the power of **hard work** and **perseverance**. Do you know what perseverance is? It means not giving up, no matter how tough things get. You might face some challenges in life—maybe school is hard or learning new skills feels frustrating—but Barry Sanders shows us that with a lot of determination, we can overcome any obstacle.

Think about when he was younger, living in Wichita, Kansas. Barry didn't come from a famous family or a wealthy background. He was just like many kids—dreaming of greatness but having to work hard to make those dreams come true. Barry had a love for football from an early age, but it wasn't always easy for him. He wasn't immediately the star. He had to put in endless hours of practice. Whether it was running drills, learning new plays, or even trying to outrun opponents in games, Barry never skipped the hard work.

And guess what? This effort paid off. He worked hard on becoming the best at what he loved, and it didn't matter if he had obstacles along the way. What mattered was his **determination** to keep going and never give up.

In his **college** years at Oklahoma State, he put in long hours, and after graduation, as a rookie with the **Detroit Lions**, Barry's work ethic stayed the same. Even though he was already incredibly skilled, Barry kept pushing himself to improve every day. Imagine how many hours of running, strength training, and practicing moves he spent. That's how hard work and perseverance help someone achieve greatness—even if the journey seems long or tough at times.

Staying True to Yourself

While hard work is important, there's something even more special about Barry Sanders. Barry's true greatness came from his ability to **stay true to himself**, even when others wanted him to be different.

In a world where everyone wants to be famous, Barry showed that it's okay to be humble. He didn't play for the flashy celebrations or the cameras. He played because he loved the game. It didn't matter how many touchdowns he scored or how many records he broke. Barry never cared about being in the spotlight—he just wanted to play football the best way he could, while respecting the game, his teammates, and the fans.

There was a time when other people tried to tell Barry to show off his success more. They told him that he should make a bigger statement with every touchdown or dance for the cameras after big plays. But Barry didn't listen to the pressure. He kept playing his way, staying focused on the game, and keeping his feet moving toward the goal. Barry Sanders believed in **authenticity**, and his decision to stay true to who he was became one of the qualities that fans admired the most.

Sometimes in life, people will try to tell you what you "should" do or how to act, but Barry's life reminds us that the most important thing is to be true to ourselves. Whether you're an athlete, a student, an artist, or someone who has big dreams, being true to your heart and staying focused on what matters will get you further than anything else.

How Barry Inspires the Next Generation

Barry Sanders' story isn't just a story about football. It's a story about someone who worked hard, stayed true to himself, and did things the right way. And you know what? His story doesn't stop with him. It continues with **you**—the next generation.

Maybe you've already tried running, playing football, or doing something else that you love, just like Barry did when he was younger. No matter what dream you have, Barry's story will remind you that you can achieve amazing things by practicing, never giving up, and being your true self.

Just think about it: Barry only played for **10 years** in the NFL, yet he's still remembered by millions of people today. His story doesn't only live in the books about football; it lives in each kid who gets inspired by his example.

Do you dream of scoring amazing touchdowns like Barry? Or maybe your dream isn't even about sports—maybe it's about art, science, music, or something completely different. Whatever your dream is, **keep working hard** and **stay true to who you are**. Like Barry, you'll go far, no matter what.

Barry Sanders' life teaches us something that will last forever: If you give everything you have to your dreams and keep believing in yourself, you'll create a legacy—just like he did. And no matter what, you'll inspire others along the way. So, the next time you feel like giving up, remember Barry Sanders. Remember that **you** have the power to achieve greatness, just like he did.

I hope you enjoyed learning about the life of Barry Sanders and the lessons he teaches. If you've liked reading about his journey from a young boy with a dream to a football legend, please consider leaving a positive review for this book on **Amazon**. Your feedback means a lot to us and helps others discover this great story.

And while you're there, be sure to check out some of our other books by simply searching for **Dale J. Gibson** on Amazon. There are even more inspiring stories to help you along your own path to greatness!

Thank you for reading, and remember: Dream big, work hard, and always stay true to who you are. You never know where your journey might take you next!

Fun Facts, Glossary and Short Quiz

Fun Facts About Barry Sanders

1. **Barry's First Love Wasn't Football!**

   Before Barry Sanders became famous for his football skills, he actually loved playing baseball. He was a talented athlete all around and even considered playing baseball professionally at one point!

2. **Barry Was Super Fast as a Kid!**

   Barry was always the fastest kid on his block in Wichita. When he was younger, his speed earned him the nickname "The Cheetah," because he could outrun almost anyone.

3. **Barry Set Crazy Records in College!**

   While playing at **Oklahoma State**, Barry set several college records, including the most rushing yards in a single season (2,628 yards in 1988). That's more than any other player at the time, and it helped him win the **Heisman Trophy**—the highest honor for a college football player.

4. **He Was Very Humble About His Achievements**

   Barry Sanders was known for never showing off after big plays.

He didn't do victory dances like other athletes. He simply handed the ball to the referee and returned to the huddle, always focused on the game.

5. **Barry Retired Very Early**

   Everyone was shocked when Barry Sanders retired in **1999** after just 10 seasons in the NFL. He was still at the top of his game! His decision to retire at such a young age was one of the biggest surprises in NFL history.

6. **Barry is One of Only a Few Who Have Run for 2,000 Yards in One Season**

   Barry's **1997** season was amazing! He rushed for **2,053 yards** in just one season, joining a rare group of only a few players in NFL history to reach that magical number.

7. **The Detroit Lions Were Lucky to Have Barry!**

   Barry Sanders played for the Detroit Lions from **1989 to 1998**. Over his ten years with the team, he became the heart and soul of the Lions and one of the best running backs in NFL history.

Glossary

- **Heisman Trophy**: A prestigious award given annually to the best college football player in the United States. Barry Sanders won this award in **1988**.

- **NFL (National Football League)**: The professional American football league where the best players from across the country compete.
- **Rushing Yards**: The total distance a player runs with the football during a game. Rushing yards are important for running backs like Barry Sanders, who often get the ball and run down the field.
- **Pro Football Hall of Fame**: A place in Canton, Ohio, where the best and most respected players in the NFL are honored after their careers.
- **MVP (Most Valuable Player)**: An award given to the player who has the best overall performance during the season in a professional sports league.
- **Perseverance**: The ability to keep working toward a goal, even when things get tough. It's about never giving up.
- **Rookie**: A player in their first year in the NFL.
- **Retire**: To stop playing professional sports after a long career. Barry Sanders retired in **1999** while still one of the best players in the league.

Quiz Time!

1. Where was Barry Sanders born?

a) Detroit, Michigan

b) Wichita, Kansas

c) Oklahoma City, Oklahoma

d) Dallas, Texas

2. What college did Barry Sanders play for?

a) University of Michigan

b) Oklahoma State University

c) University of Alabama

d) Stanford University

3. What prestigious award did Barry Sanders win in 1988?

a) NFL MVP

b) Heisman Trophy

c) Rookie of the Year

d) Super Bowl MVP

4. What team did Barry Sanders play for in the NFL?

a) Green Bay Packers

b) Dallas Cowboys

c) Detroit Lions

d) Chicago Bears

5. How many yards did Barry Sanders rush for during the 1997 NFL season?

a) 1,200 yards

b) 2,000 yards

c) 1,500 yards

d) 2,053 yards

6. When did Barry Sanders retire from the NFL?

a) 1997

b) 1999

c) 2002

d) 2004

7. What nickname did Barry Sanders have when he was a kid?

a) The Lightning Bolt

b) The Cheetah

c) The Panther

d) The Eagle

8. What does the Pro Football Hall of Fame honor?

a) Players with the most points

b) The best football teams

c) The greatest players in NFL history

d) The longest touchdown runs

Quiz Answers:

1. b) Wichita, Kansas
2. b) Oklahoma State University
3. b) Heisman Trophy
4. c) Detroit Lions
5. d) 2,053 yards
6. b) 1999
7. b) The Cheetah
8. c) The greatest players in NFL history

Thank you for checking out these **Fun Facts**, **Glossary** terms, and taking part in the **Quiz**! We hope you learned even more about the incredible journey of **Barry Sanders**. Remember—whether on the field, in school, or in life, hard work, perseverance, and staying true to yourself are key to achieving greatness!

If you enjoyed this book, don't forget to leave a positive review on **Amazon**. Your thoughts help us reach more readers and share inspiring stories like Barry's with the world. And be sure to check out other books by **Dale J. Gibson** by searching for his name on **Amazon**. We have many more stories to share with you!

Made in the USA
Monee, IL
11 April 2025